ZOOM CITY

Rob Alcraft

ILLUSTRATED BY
Jonathan Adams

Heinemann Library
Des Plaines, Illinois

© 1999 Reed Educational & Professional Publishing
Published by Heinemann Library, an imprint of Reed Educational & Professional Publishing,
1350 East Touhy Avenue, Suite 240 West, Des Plaines, IL 60018

Designed by Paul Cooper
Cover illustrated by Michael Fisher
Printed in Hong Kong by Wing King Tong Co. Ltd.

03 02 01 00 99
10 9 8 7 6 5 4 3 2 1

Library of Congress Cataloging-in-Publication Data

Alcraft, Rob, 1966–
      Zoom City / Rob Alcraft; illustrated by Jonathan Adams.
          Includes Index p. cm.
      Summary: Depicts a city and its buildings, streets, underground,
and activities, beginning with an aerial view and descending to the
microscopic level, Sidebars present unusual facts and focus on
specific cities such as Tokyo, Vienna, and London.
      ISBN 1-57572-717-X (library binding)
      1. Cities and Towns--Juvenile literature.   2. Cities and towns-
-Pictorial works--Juvenile literature.   [1. Cities and towns.
2. City and town life.] I.Adams, Jon (Jonathan), ill. II. Title.
HT152.A43   1998
307.76--dc21   98-11592
                                                              CIP
                                                               AC

Yᴏu are beginning a journey. You will travel from the limits of space to the depths of Zoom City. Every page will draw you deeper into an incredible world. There are facts to amaze you and hidden events that only you will find.

You will see the earth from the eye of a satellite and speed past towering skyscrapers. You will whiz through the darkness of the subway and go beyond to the deep sewers and subterranean places. You will explore the sprawling mechanical world of buildings and feel the pulse of the City's electronic heart.

In a single day of twists and turns you can discover hidden worlds. Glimpse invisible creatures in a magnified empire of the mini-beasts. See the dust mites crawling, at this moment, on your skin.

The secrets of Zoom City are waiting.

CONTENTS

SATELLITE EYE

It rains. In the atmosphere high above the City, a storm has gathered. Lightning flashes across the sky at temperatures five times hotter than the surface of the sun.

From space the electronic eye of a satellite watches the storm move across the City. It beams pictures to Earth. At 6 a.m., on the morning news, the City people watch the storm through the satellite eye. Other news arrives from space of a forest fire begun by lightning. We can see it as a tiny but growing glow, burning in the distance.

From high in the sky we can see the curve of the earth as the sun rises. The City seems so small. It is little more than a spot, nestling near the mountains and the blue of the sea.

Storm power

A single thunderstorm can release 130 million gallons of water and discharge enough heat to supply electrical power to the entire U.S.A. for 20 minutes. A full-blown hurricane is 12,000 times more powerful.

Striking lightning

At any one time around the globe, there are 2,000 thunderstorms taking place. The earth is hit by lightning a staggering 100 times a second.

Meteorites and toilet waste

About 19,000 meteorites hit the earth every year. The chances of being hit are tiny, and most of us are more at risk from "blue ice"— frozen waste from airline toilets.

High speed space junk

There are about 7,000 large pieces of space junk orbiting the earth—including bits of rockets and satellites—all traveling at 17,000 miles per hour.

THE CITY

The storm rolls into the distance. Now we see the City. A web of streets and highways reach out into the countryside. In a generation, this city has grown 20 times bigger. It has spread, swallowing villages and towns around it.

Hidden in the center is the old City where the streets are a chaotic maze. There are alleys and tall buildings crammed together. These old streets were built before cars and are wide enough only for carts and carriages.

This City is a living thing, a home to millions of people. There is culture, action, and entertainment existing beside work and traffic. There are schools and riches and people of every race. Almost anything you want is here and some things you do not. Welcome to the City.

Biggest city

The biggest city in the world is Tokyo in Japan. The next biggest is Mexico City, Mexico. Both of these cities probably have more than 20 million people—if you include the whole suburban area.

More, bigger, more

London needs an area equal to all the productive land in the United Kingdom—that's an area 125 times its own size—for supplies such as food and to absorb its pollution.

Mega cities

Five hundred years ago—a mere blip in human history—only five cities had populations of more than 100,000. Now there are about 300 cities with populations of more than a million people.

Urban heat bubbles

Cities can change climates. They are hot. Concrete and bricks soak up heat from the sun, and cars and industry generate heat. This raises the temperature 2 to 4 degrees above the temperature of the surrounding land.

THE PORT

This is the river that flows through the City. See it now, a wide waterway, surrounded by docks and warehouses. It is running fast, swollen by rain and tidal water rushing up from the sea. On its bank, firefighters battle to put out a blaze.

Ships and tankers tie up at the docks. They carry bananas from the Americas, and cocoa, coffee, and tea from Africa and Asia. There are cars, cloth, and machinery. All of it is loaded and unloaded by giant cranes— some with long legs and wheels that look like mechanical ballet dancers.

There is a constant stream of ships. Small, powerful boats called tugs help the larger ships steer up river. Police and customs officials patrol, searching for smuggled goods and drugs and even stowaways.

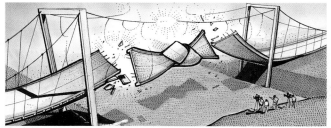

The collapsing bridge
All tall buildings and bridges have to be designed to be safe in storms. The Tacoma Narrows Bridge in Washington was open only four months when a freak wind set it swaying wildly. Within a few hours, it had collapsed.

Supertanker
Some ships are now so big that many ports, and even the Panama Canal, are too small to take them. Some supertankers are heavier than the largest skyscrapers!

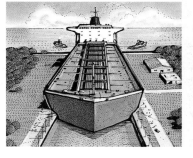

Shrinking world
In 1849, the journey from New York to San Francisco took 146 days. Now you can hop onto a scheduled airline, and it takes 6 hours and 20 minutes.

The hungry city
Cities occupy only 2% of the world's land, but they contain more than 40% of the world's people and use 75% of the world's resources.

SKY HIGH

Three hundred feet (one hundred meters) in the air, people are working on the building. Look down and the view is dizzying. At this height, the building moves slightly in the wind. It is a skyscraper designed to sway a little, because this will help it withstand storms and earthquakes.

The building and rebuilding of the City is endless. Business demands more space and the buildings have grown ever higher to produce it. Now one piece of land is multiplied many times over as skyscrapers soar 50 stories into the air.

A building like this can cost millions of dollars and consume many thousands of tons of concrete, glass, and steel. In the endless quest to build higher, new ways of building are invented and reinvented. The race is on to build skyscrapers faster, taller, cheaper.

What price?

In Tokyo, Japan, competition for land has pushed prices sky high. A piece of prime land the size of this page could cost you more than $20,000!

Skyscrapers

The world's tallest buildings are the Petronas Towers (above) in Kuala Lumpur, Malaysia, at 1,483 feet. (452 meters) But not for long—a building planned for Shanghai, China will beat them by just 26 feet (8 meters)! For comparison, New York's Empire State Building is about 1,247 feet (380 meters) high and the Eiffel Tower in Paris reaches 985 feet (300 meters).

Money, money, money

Cities are centers of business and trade. Unimaginably huge sums of money change hands. Trading in money alone (between cities like London, New York, and Tokyo) is estimated to amount to 1 trillion dollars a day.

Hungry Vienna

Constant building is making the Austrian city of Vienna fat. It gets 40,000 tons heavier every day.

RUSH HOUR

Move it. It's 8 a.m. and time to rush—to work, to shop, to school. To get there is everything. And to do it, we all squeeze into the same small City space at exactly the same moment. It is rush hour.

The City needs this daily injection of people, work and money. It needs rush hour. Its businesses, restaurants, and entertainments thrive on it.

But the sheer numbers of cars and people bring problems. Traffic inches along at the speed of a horse-drawn carriage. Lines of cars spew out exhaust fumes. The people inside seethe angrily. Pollution—the smoke and gas from cars and industry—lies in a thick blanket over the City. But the rush goes on. The City swells with people.

Car crazy

We just love our cars—and there are many to love. We have 500 million of them. In fact, the residents of Los Angeles love cars so much that they drive a combined distance of 140 million miles (225 kilometers) a day—enough to get them to Mars.

Weather warning

We've created a new weather condition. It's called smog. In cities like Los Angeles and Mexico City, pollution from cars and industry combine to form freak clouds of murky brown mist. Asthma and other breathing difficulties have increased.

Cars while you sleep

Worldwide, a new car is produced every second. Go to bed tonight, and, by the time you wake up, another 30,000 new cars will have been made.

Grocery cart victims

On average, five Americans are seriously injured by supermarket carts every hour.

Road to nowhere

Hong Kong has the greatest density of cars in any city. So many in fact that each car has only 12 feet (3.59 meters) of road.

UNDER YOUR FEET

This is a street. It is like a skin. It covers a crisscross of pipes and cables linking all parts of the City. Electricity surges from power stations to offices. Pipes pump water to a million homes. Fiber optic cables carry information as light beams, to and fro. Telephone cables babble with electronic voices.

But a cable is cut. Part of the City dies. Computer screens, telephones, and TVs go silent. Lights flicker and go dead.

The people with backhoes and drills are like the City's doctors. They treat and replace aging pipes, laying new networks to revive the City.

Telephone chatter

On an average day Londoners make about 18 million telephone calls. That's at least 600 new calls in the time it has taken you to read this.

Alligators

In some U.S. cities, animals as large as alligators have made their homes in the sewers and waterways that flow beneath our homes and streets.

What happens when you flush?

Did you know that brushing your teeth with the water running uses 3 gallons (10 liters) of water? This is more water than some people have for an entire day. About one third of all our water goes straight down the drain!

Drink the river dry

Los Angeles consumes more than 11.1 million cubic yards (8.5 million cubic meters) of water every day. In the 1980s, it began to draw supplies from the Colorado River. The once mighty flow now no longer reaches the sea.

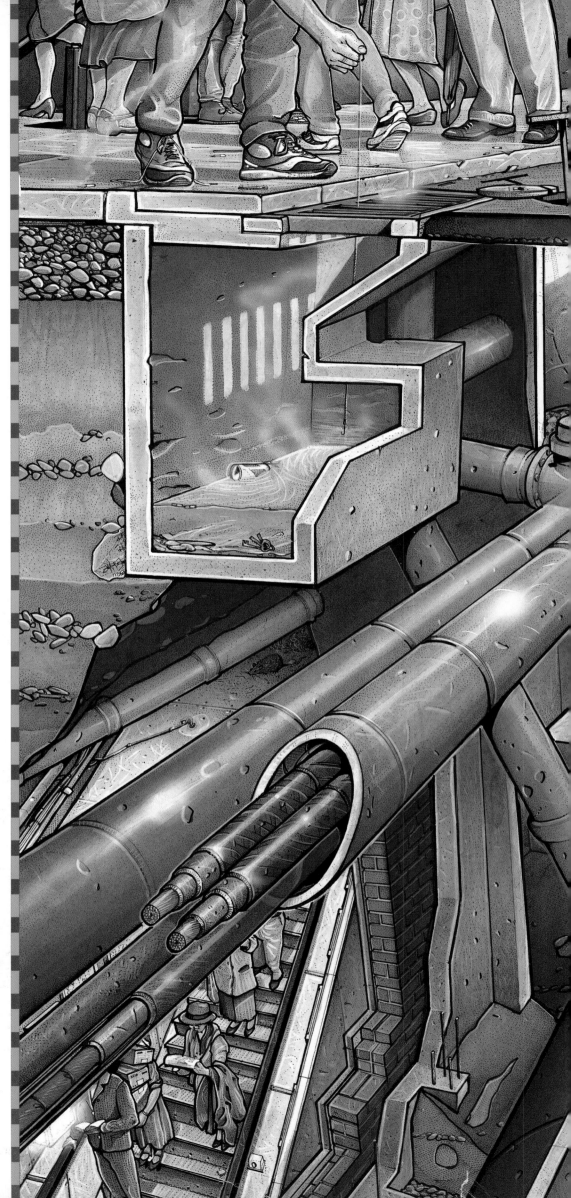

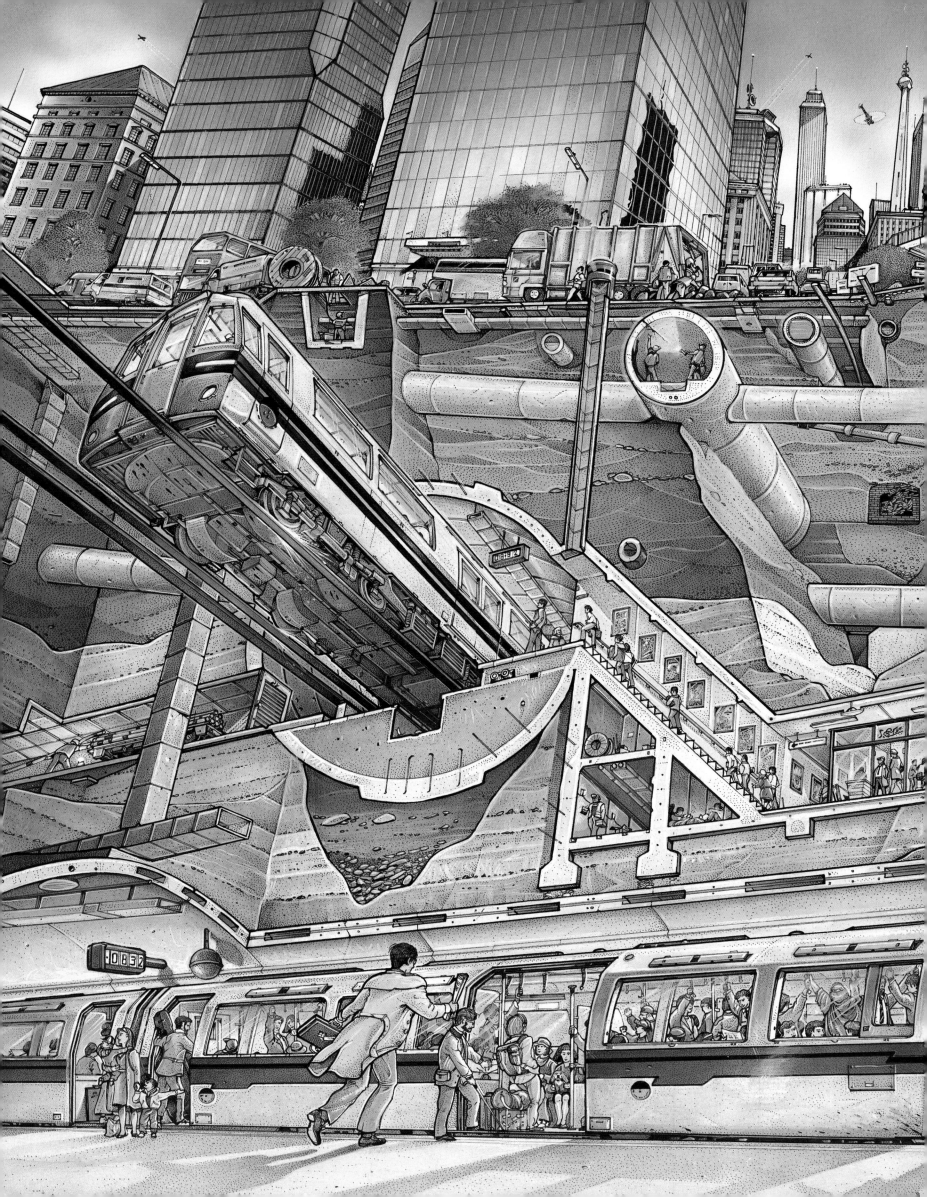

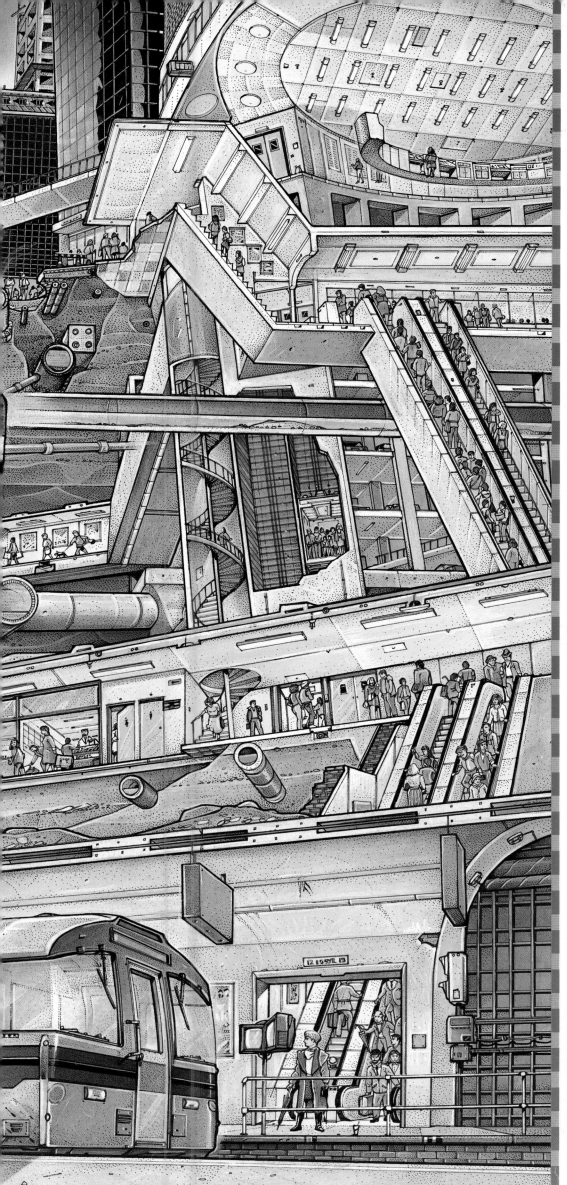

SUBCITY

Now deep beneath your feet is a subterranean world of tunnels and sewers. Subway stations share the soil with the remains of past civilizations and pipes.

Down here are the City's roots—the foundations of buildings. To hold up the skyscrapers, there are concrete pillars driven down through the soil and rock. Layers of stone and brick support the weight of buildings above.

There is life in this underground world. Rats outnumber us nine to one. And there are people—millions of them squeezed into rush hour subway trains—whizzing through the darkness. What else can you see?

Going underground

New York has one of the world's busiest subways. Opened in 1868, it now carries more than 7 million passengers a day. That's enough people to fill 60 large football stadiums.

Ads galore

By the age of 18, the average American has seen more than 250,000 advertisements.

The Great Stink

In the hot summer of 1858, the smell of London's raw sewage flowing into the Thames River forced government officials to abandon the Houses of Parliament. Fortunately, most cities now at least partially treat sewage.

Subway sardines

Tokyo's subway gets so busy that special rush hour platform guards are employed. They squeeze people into the train and push the doors closed.

UNDERWORLD

We go deeper still. Here there are the bones of dinosaurs or the fossil imprints of plants and insects many thousands of years old. There could be a medieval burial crypt, skeletons, and ruins. It's all there. Dig and you will find it.

Very few cities have survived intact from the past. Nearly all have been destroyed by fire or war. Down here, hundreds of years of history are piled on top of each other as new buildings and streets are built over the old.

Each layer holds the secrets of those who built it. From the foundations of houses, we can see how these people lived. From what they left behind, we can see perhaps what they ate or what they believed. From their skeletons, we can often tell how they died, what diseases they had, and even what they looked like.

Digging for history
Archaeologists can find out a surprising amount from what they dig up. Did you know that the world's first pottery was made in Japan 14,000 years ago? Or that the world's first battery was made about 2,000 years ago in Iraq?

Ancient cities
Ancient Rome was the world's first megacity. By A.D. 100 it probably contained a million people. The mystery is why so many ancient cities declined. Some may have been destroyed in war. Others may have overused the farm land that fed them.

Rat athletics
Rats are athletes. They can stay afloat for 72 hours, jump more than 6 feet (2 meters), and run a 100 meter race in fewer than 10 seconds. They have also been known to swim in the pipes of a toilet to get into a house.

Life after death
As a modern human, full of preservatives and chemicals absorbed from food and water, you will take longer to decompose than your ancestors.

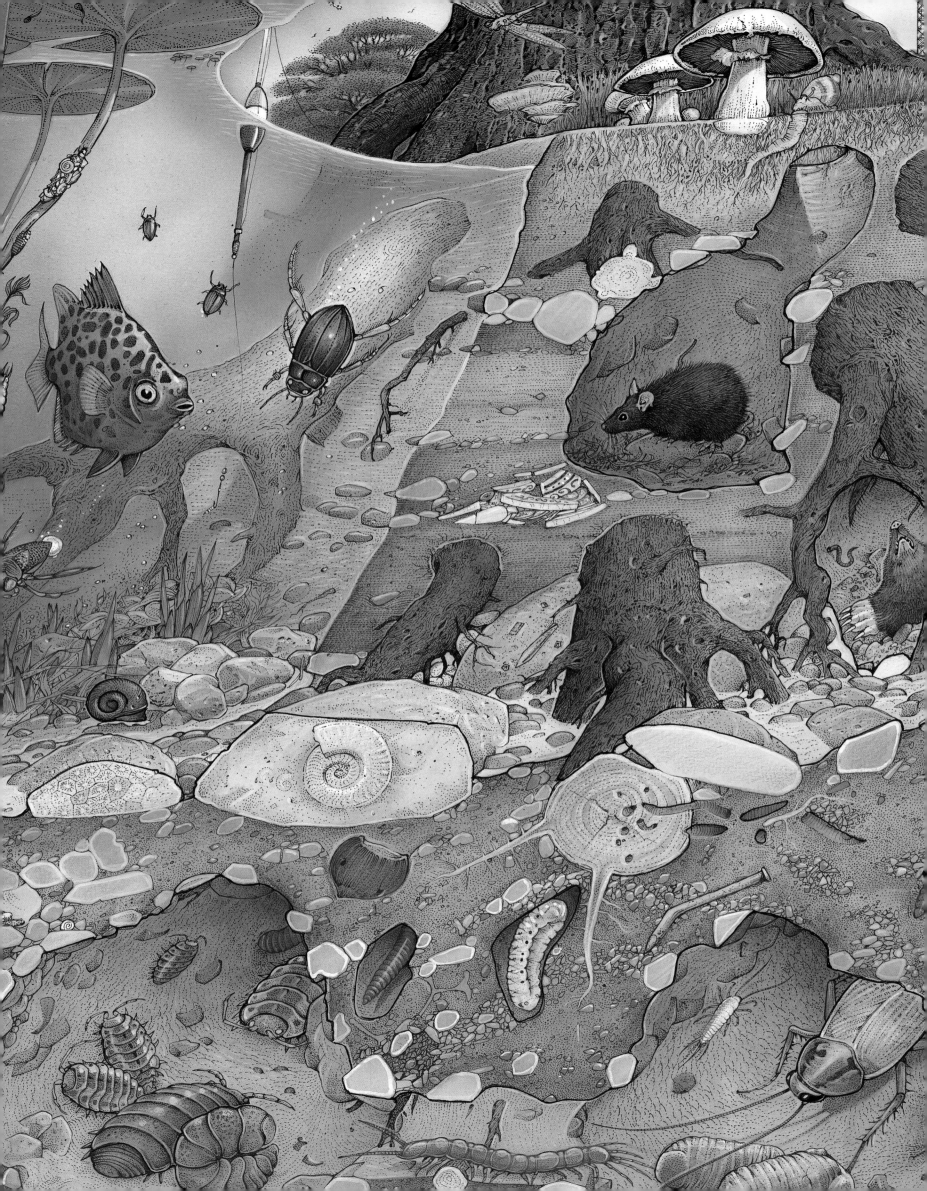

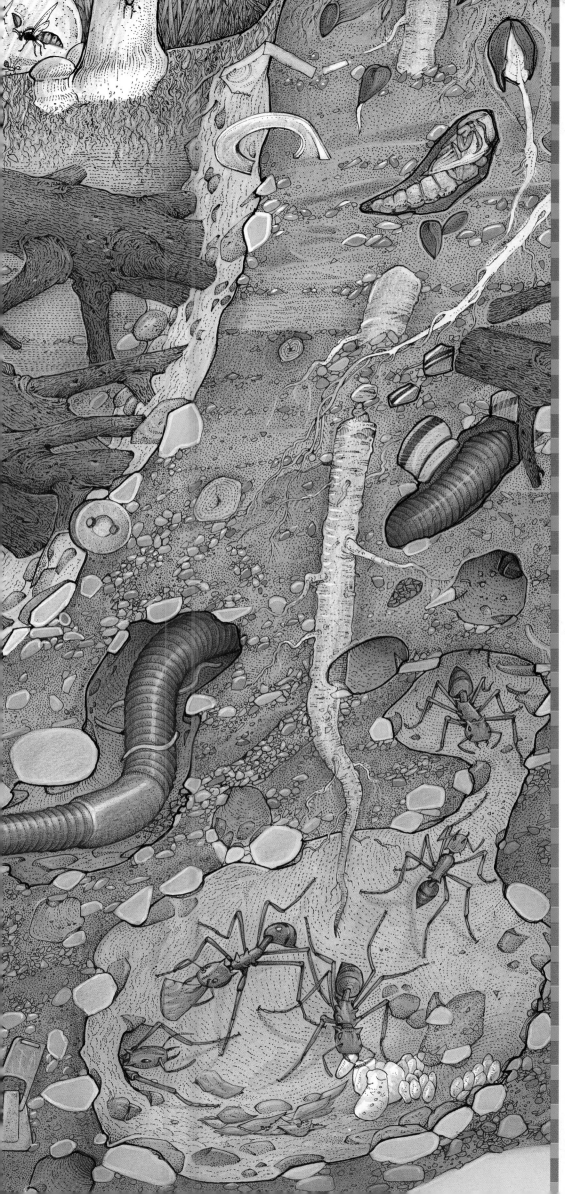

SECRET LIFE

This is a world of soil and damp, where ants raise aphids just like we raise cattle, and near-blind moles forage for slugs and worms to eat.

Hold a handful of this soil. Among the tiny rock fragments and pieces of plants and animals, live millions of bacteria and fungi. These tiny organisms attack and rot all dead things—turning them into food from which new plants can grow.

This soil is the place where seeds wait. Each seed has a code that is cracked only by the right combination of temperature and water. Once unlocked they grow quickly. Roots push through the soil at up to 4/100 of an inch per hour and produce pressures strong enough to break concrete. Given the chance, these seeds will reclaim the City for themselves.

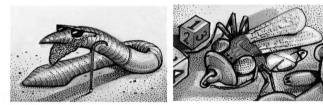

Long live the worm
Did you know that an earthworm can live up to 10 years and even the humble snail can live 5 years? Male houseflies are less lucky, usually managing only 18 days.

Remember bee
A bee's brain—the size of a grain of sugar—is the ultimate micromachine. Navigating by the sun, bees can remember the type and color of flowers and also the time of day the flowers open.

Ant matter
If all the species on Earth —including ourselves— were weighed, 10% of the entire weight would be ants.

Long live the seed
Seeds will outlive us all. They can grow thousands of years after lying dormant in the soil. The oldest seeds on record to grow were at least 10,000 years old—6,000 years older than Stonehenge. They were Arctic lupins found frozen in mud.

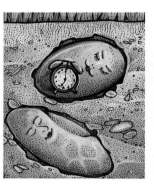

NO ESCAPE

The mini-beasts and insects already have control in the tiny jungle-world of your carpet. Even in the cleanest houses they patrol the baseboards and under your bed. They scurry up pipes and hide in corners.

Some are so small that they will live, breed, and die, and you will never see them. These are organisms like microscopic bacteria that grow by the millions on damp walls and tiny dust mites that feast on flakes of your dead skin. Insects—like bedbugs and mosquitoes—drink your blood, sucking it up through a long spike on their heads.

And talk about dirt! Pollen from plants, bits of earth, and the debris of dead insect bodies settle everywhere.

You are not alone

For every human there are 200 to 300 million individual insects. That is 10,000 insects per square yard (meter) of land— right where you are now.

Bloodsuckers

Mosquitoes are feared because they suck human blood and carry the deadly diseases malaria and yellow fever. Every year, over two million people die from malaria. Only female mosquitoes feed on blood. The males eat plants.

We will survive

Cockroaches are survivors. They have proved impossible to eliminate and can even live for up to a week with their heads cut off. They are also the fastest insects on legs and can run at 5 feet (1.5 meters) per second.

Skin

Over your lifetime you will shed nearly 44 pounds (20 kilograms) of dead skin. No surprise then that about 90% of house dust is you and your family's skin.

Fast breeders

If one pair of fruit flies were to breed free from death, disease, and predators for one year, the resulting fly generations would form a ball larger than 87 million miles across (140 million kilometers). That's the distance from here to the sun.

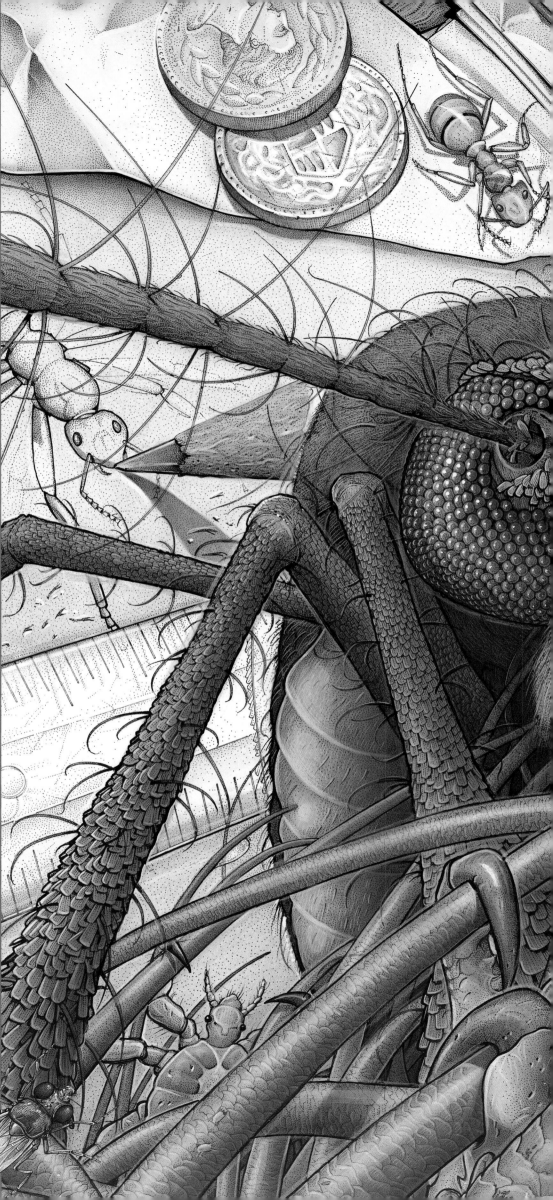

THE BEDROOM

Of the strange collection of creatures in your bedroom, the strangest is you.

You will spend 27 years of your life in bed, 8 years watching television, and another 6 years eating, washing, and brushing your teeth. Your toenails will grow 8 feet (2.5 meters), and your hair 30 feet (9 meters). You will shed nearly 44 pounds (20 kilograms) of dead skin flakes, and produce 3,700 gallons (14,000 liters) of sweat.

And, while you're doing this, you will eat 7 tons of bread and potatoes, more than 5,000 bananas, and 893 chickens. Unless of course you're a vegetarian, in which case your lifetime consumption of nuts will be considerably more than the average of 330 pounds (150 kilograms).

And this is all just you. Many cities have more than 5 million inhabitants, all eating their way through mountains of food or spending several lifetimes each day just brushing their teeth.

Aaah-chooooooo!
Clean your room and the dust will make you sneeze. A sneezing nose forces out air at about 90 miles (150 kilometers) per hour, a wind speed greater than most hurricanes.

Lost bones
You were born with more than 800 bones, but many join together as you grow. You now have 206. Nearly half of them are in your hands and feet.

The tube
It takes two major power plants just to power Britain's 38.3 million household televisions. An audience of 17 million soap opera fans needs a major power plant all to itself.

Mmm is for mouthwash
Until the 17th century, urine was recommended as an early morning mouthwash. Its slightly acidic qualities were supposed to neutralize unpleasant nighttime secretions.

THE PARK

The park is busy at the end of the day. Kids kick soccer balls. Joggers keep fit. Dogs are walked. This is the place to escape, to play tennis, or to swing on swings. Or you can just watch as mountain bikers, skateboarders, and inline skaters whizz by.

But the real action in the park has been going on unseen. There is a chemical at work. It is so important that we could not live without it.

The chemical is chlorophyll—a word that means "green leaf." All green plants contain this chemical and use it to make food from sunlight. They store this food in roots and leaves. Animals, insects, bacteria, and fungi feed on it. All life—including us—depend on the sun to provide fuel for plants.

None of the rush and bustle of the City, none of the work, none of the buildings would be possible without the plants.

Little weathermen

Some people claim you can tell the temperature by a cricket's chirp. You're supposed to count the number of chirps in a 14 second period and add that number to 40. They say it gives you the right answer 75% of the time.

Trees are cool

Trees keep our parks cool. Every day a tree sweats out the equivalent of about 2.5 bathtubs of cooling water.

Fast-moving mushroom

One of the world's fastest growing plants is a mushroom. The Lady in the Veil grows 4/10 of an inch (10 millimeters) a minute to its full height of 8 inches (200 millimeters).

Fanatical fans

Humans are the only animals that have invented sports. Over 250,000 people watched the chariot races in ancient Rome. Nowadays, more than a billion people watch different sports events on television.

Forgotten people

Not everyone in cities finds life easy. Many people are poor or out of work. One estimate puts the number of homeless people in the United States at 760,000.

NIGHT

Night falls and lights glimmer. At home, people reach for switches and buttons. Millions of TVs and microwave ovens snap on. Power stations run at full stretch to meet the surging demand for electricity.

Over the river, fireworks explode. Restaurants fill with people. Cultures from all over the world collide, fuse, and mix. There are rhythms from South America, the Caribbean, and Africa, food from India and the Middle East. There is sport, theater, movies, and dancing. This is reason enough to put up with the City's noise and dirt.

Night deepens. People will work on to prepare for tomorrow's rush. For others, there is sleep. Breathing and pulse rates slow. Body temperatures drop.

The City sleeps.

Sleepwalkers' convention
The world sleepwalkers' convention created havoc at a hotel in Sydney, Australia in 1994. People at the conference caused thousands of dollars of damage wandering around during the night.

The Dracula hormone

Darkness is a signal for a gland to produce a hormone called melatonin—the "Dracula hormone"—which triggers sleep. Some blind people who can't recognize darkness are always tired.

Urban future
Fifty million people lived in cities in 1800. That's less than the present population of the United Kingdom. By the year 2000 there will be 3 billion people living in cities. For the first time in human history, we will be an urban species.

Future fear

People have always feared the unknown. At the dawn of the railway age, when trains began to be faster than horses, people feared that traveling faster than 12 miles per hour would affect the minds of passengers.

DID YOU SEE...?

Now you have zoomed through the City, what did you see? Did you see the rushing fire emergency services, the traffic accident, and a hidden moth? Look now and see if you saw these mystery objects. There is a clue with each object that might help your search. Happy zooming.

Watch out for the flashing lights of the fire engine. You must get out of its way, but can you find it first? Keep your eyes open for any others.

You wouldn't see pollen like this unless it was magnified.

What is this backhoe building?

This moth is an expert at using camouflage to hide itself. It's almost impossible to see, but can you find it?

Were you witness to this crime?

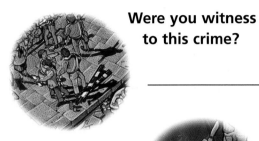
Someone might get a nasty surprise down in the sewers.

About 30 years ago, someone buried this time capsule to be opened in the year 2000. What objects would you put in a time capsule to be opened in 2050?

You'd see this forest fire from a satellite. A forest fire can have many causes, such as a flash of lightning, a piece of glass concentrating the sun's rays, or a cigarette carelessly thrown away.

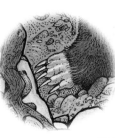
Somewhere underground you'd see this hand and its furry owner. Even near the centers of cities, many types of animals can find places to make their homes.

This meteorite came from outer space. Did you see it hurtle by?

Will this flowerpot hit anyone in the rush?

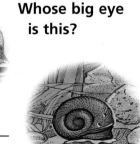
Whose big eye is this?

Did you see this tiger in someone's bedroom?

Where is the water snail?

There are many forms of transportation in a city. Can you find this helicopter and a police officer on a horse?

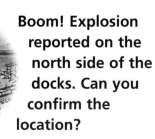
Boom! Explosion reported on the north side of the docks. Can you confirm the location?

Who's playing cat and mouse?

ACKNOWLEDGMENTS

The City information in this book has been compiled from a range of sources. Thanks to the following books and other sources for providing inspiration for the fascinating facts.

Satellite Eye
Storm power: *Storm*, Planet Earth, ABC Whipple, Time Life books, Amsterdam, 1982. **Striking lightning:** *Savage Skies*, Bill Jones and Liz Mcleod, Granada Television 1996 and *Storm*, Planet Earth, ABC Whipple, Time Life books, Amsterdam, 1982. **High speed space junk:** *Guardian Education*, February 14, 1995.

The City
Biggest city: *Top Ten of Everything*, Russell, Ash, Dorling Kindersley, 1994. **More, bigger, more:** *Independent on Sunday*, April 14, 1996. **Mega cities:** *The Real World*, ed. Bruce Marshall, Marshall Editions Developments, 1991 and *Dictionary of World History*, Nelson.

The Port
The hungry city: *Independent on Sunday*, April 14, 1996.

Sky High
Skyscrapers: Various, including *Guinness Book of Records*, Guinness Publishing, 1997. **Money, money, money:** *Guardian Education*, March 7, 1995. **Hungry Vienna:** *Independent on Sunday*, April 14, 1996.

Rush Hour
Cars while you sleep: *Gaia Atlas of Cities*, Herbert Girardet, Gaia Books Ltd 1992. **Grocery cart victims:** *The Real Facts of Life 1994*, Rowland Morgan, Earthscan 1994.

Under your Feet
Telephone chatter: BT Press Office, London. **Drink the river dry:** *The Real World*, ed. Bruce Marshall, Marshall Editions Developments Ltd, 1991.

Subcity
Ads galore: *The Real Facts of Life 1994*, Rowland Morgan, Earthscan, 1994.

Underworld
Ancient cities: *Gaia Atlas of Cities*, Herbert Girardet, Gaia Books Ltd, 1992.

Secret Life
Long live the worm: *Extraordinary Animals*, Marcus Schneck, The Apple Press 1990. **Ant matter:** *The Real Facts of Life 1994*, Rowland Morgan, Earthscan, 1994. **Long live the seed:** *Guinness Book of Records,* Guinness Publishing, *1995.*

No Escape
You are not alone: I*nsects of the Northern Hemisphere*, George C McGavin, Dragon's World Books, 1992. **Skin:** *Hidden Worlds: The Human Body*, Heather Amery and Jane Songi, Heinemann, 1993. **Fast breeders:** *Insects of the Northern Hemisphere*, George C McGavin, Dragon's World Books, 1992.

The Bedroom
Aaah-choooooo!: *Hidden Worlds: The Human Body*, Heather Amery and Jane Songi, Heinemann, 1993. **Lost bones:** *Hidden Worlds: The Human Body*, Heather Amery and Jane Songi, Heinemann, 1993. **The tube:** *The Real Facts of Life 1994*, Rowland Morgan, Earthscan, 1994. **Mmm is for mouthwash:** Various, including Radio 4 "And I'm the Queen of Sheba," Thursday, October 10, 1996 and—with variations—*Guinness Book of Oddities*, Geoff Tibballs, Guinness Publishing Ltd, 1995.

The Park
Little weathermen: *Savage Skies*, Bill Jones and Liz Mcleod, Granada Television, 1996. **Trees are cool:** *Gaia Atlas of Cities*, Herbert Girardet, Gaia Books Ltd, 1992. **Fast-moving mushroom:** *Guinness Book of Oddities*, Geoff Tibballs, Guinness Publishing Ltd, 1995.

Night
Sleepwalkers' convention: Various, including *The Guardian*, Saturday, July 13, 1996. **The Dracula hormone:** *Guardian Education*, October 5, 1993. **Future fear:** Various, including *Guinness Book of Oddities*, Geoff Tibballs, Guinness Publishing Ltd, 1995.

THE WORLD'S GIANT CITIES

The world is dotted with cities. These are the cities with the biggest populations. (Figures are for urban areas, compiled from census data and estimates.)

TOKYO, Japan: 25,000,000

NEW YORK CITY: 18,000,000

SÃO PAULO, Brazil: 18,000,000

MEXICO CITY, Mexico: 15,000,000

LOS ANGELES: 14,500,000

SHANGHAI, China: 13,500,000

CAIRO, Egypt: 13,300,000

BOMBAY, India: 12,600,000

BUENOS AIRES, Argentina: 12,600,000

RIO DE JANEIRO, Brazil: 11,200,000

OTHER MAJOR CITIES
PARIS, France: 9,063,000
LONDON, England: 7,926,000
BERLIN, Germany: 3,590,000

INDEX